Ten First Steps on the Internet
A Learning Journey for Teachers

M. D. Roblyer
University of West Georgia

Merrill
Prentice Hall

Upper Saddle River, New Jersey
Columbus, Ohio

Vice President and Publisher: Jeffery W. Johnston
Editor: Debra A. Stollenwerk
Development Editor: Gianna Marsella
Editorial Assistant: Penny S. Burleson
Production Editor: JoEllen Gohr
Production Manager: Pamela D. Bennett
Director of Marketing: Kevin Flanagan
Marketing Manager: Amy June
Marketing Services Manager: Krista Groshong

10 9 8 7 6 5 4 3 2
ISBN 0-13-030502-2

ॐ

Table of Contents

Dedication

for Marilyn Comet—
educational technology luminary, great lady, great friend

Preface

Why This Book Was Written

The most enduring metaphor for the Internet is that of a highway, perhaps because it is such an appropriate comparison. Highways, like the Internet, can be paths to adventure and new knowledge, ways to get quickly to destinations already known, and courses to wander casually in search of new discoveries.

However, either the paved roads of a countryside or the electronic pathways of the World Wide Web also can be a confusing collection of perplexing signs and symbols, places to get lost and frustrated, a series of dead ends. The difference between these two experiences is understanding the basics of "travel" and the resources available to help the traveler.

Many educators are beginning to recognize how important it is to "get out on the road" and begin learning a new way for themselves and their students to see the world. This book is designed to be an easy way for them to learn some of the basics required to become a skilled "Internet traveler." An old proverb holds that a journey of a thousand miles begins with but a single step. This booklet has a series of ten "first steps" to get educators started on what could be a most enlightening journey.

What You Need to Prepare for the Trip

Before setting out on a journey, some preparation always is in order. However, you needn't learn everything at once. One of the best things about the Internet is that you don't have to be a very technical person to use it, just as you need not be an auto mechanic to drive a car! At first, teachers may want to ask someone to prepare their "vehicle" for them to get them started. Later, they can learn more technical items about Internet use so they don't have to rely as much on others.

But not even the best driver's manual can substitute for driving experience; getting out on the Internet is the best way to learn it. Before you start, though, be sure you have obtained the following **two** items.

❶ An Internet-ready computer. Any veteran traveler knows that having a well-equipped vehicle can make all the difference in the quality of a trip, and so it is with the Internet. To make your Internet travel go smoothly, make sure you have a computer:

RAM is the memory that holds programs while they are being used.

☛ *With fast enough speed and enough Random Access Memory (RAM) to do Internet tasks:*

Good: 100 MHz speed, 32 Megabytes (MB) RAM
Better: 300 MHz speed, 64 MB RAM
Best: 600 MHz or better speed, 128 MB RAM

☛ *Equipped with a fast enough connection:*

Speed at which signals are sent between computers is measured in bits per second, or bps.

Good: A computer with a 28.8 thousand bits per second (bps) modem, and connected to a telephone or ISDN line

Better: A computer with a 56 thousand bps modem, and connected to a telephone or ISDN line, or to a cable modem

Best: A computer on a network that is connected to the Internet with T1 or ISDN lines or by cable modem

☛ *Equipped with browser software.* Browsers are programs that display web pages as pictures so you can look at ("browse") through them and do tasks with them. The most common web browsers are:

Netscape Communicat

Internet Explorer ‹

• *Netscape Communicator*

• Microsoft's *Internet Explorer*

However, companies such as America Online have their own browsers. Each of these browsers has versions for Windows PC and Macintosh computers.

In this book, we will show screen examples with *Netscape Communicator*, although others are similar. Below is an example of the Prentice Hall web site as viewed through the *Netscape Communicator* browser.

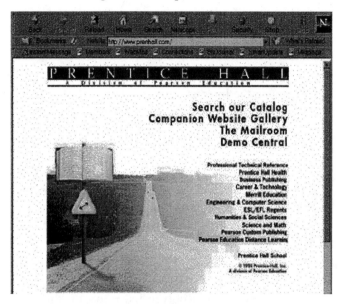

Netscape Browser Displaying the Prentice Hall Web Site

❷ **An Internet connection.** Next, you need to be connected to the Internet. What exactly does it mean to be "connected?" Although there are several different ways, they all mean you are able to use browser software to have your Internet-ready computer send electronic signals over lines and make contact with other Internet-ready computers. But access to the Internet is not free. Even schools or districts that provide it free to their teachers must pay someone for it. If you have no group that provides access for you, shop for the best Internet provider. Look for three things when you shop for a provider:

Reliability:	Can you get on the Internet whenever you want? Or is the line busy or is the provider's computer "down" a lot of the time?
Good support:	Is someone available 24 hours a day to help you if you have problems or questions?
Fair price:	Is there a reasonable flat fee, or do they charge by the minute?

If you have an Internet-ready computer and a connection to the Internet, you are ready to begin the ten steps in this book!

How to Use This Book

Appropriate for use in a lab setting, *Ten First Steps on the Internet: A Learning Journey for Teachers* takes a step-by-step approach to helping you learn how to navigate the Internet and use it as a powerful resource for teaching and learning.

Written as a companion to the Merrill textbook *Integrating Educational Technology into Teaching,* 2nd Edition, by Roblyer and Edwards, this book expands on the information in chapter 8 (*Integrating the Internet into Education*) and extends coverage of integrating the Internet into content area teaching discussed in chapters 10-15.

In addition, this handbook highlights lesson plans from the CD-ROM that use Internet strategies to further help users effectively integrate Internet technologies into teaching.

Because this handbook encourages hands-on Internet experiences, students can complete activities using the online "Try This!" Tutorial on the companion website for the textbook, located at

http://www.prenhall.com/roblyer

Look for the following icons or pictures to help guide you through each of the 10 sections:

This "book" icon at the beginning of each section signals new Internet terms you will want to learn.

This "light bulb" icon marks "helpful hints" or additional explanation to help you understand the new information.

Try This!

http://www.prenhall. com/roblyer

Look for this "companion website" image throughout each section to mark "Try This!" exercises for you to check your learning at each step. These Internet exercises can be completed using the online "Try This!" Tutorial on the companion website, located at **http://www.prenhall.com/roblyer**

Page numbers mentioned in this book are from *Integrating Educational Technology into Teaching,* 2nd Edition (or *IETT*), by Roblyer and Edwards.

Enjoy the trip!

Acknowledgments

Many people look upon writing a book as an impossible undertaking. In fact, it is. But what they may not realize is how similar an enterprise it is to what classroom teachers do every day. Both involve accomplishing tasks with too little time, resources, and knowledge. Both require commitment and sacrifice: time taken away from family and friends and long hours without adequate rest or "down time." Both have teaching as their purpose and learning as their ultimate goal. But perhaps most important, both teachers and writers must love their work to make it all worth it.

My thanks go out once more to all the people who make it possible for me to do what I love. For this book, I am obliged especially to recognize my continuing debt to my friend, mentor, and editor Debbie Stollenwerk; other Merrill professionals Gianna Marsella, Heather Fraser, and Penny Burleson; my family, Bill and Paige Wiencke and Becky Kelley; and friends such as Sherry Alter and Paul Belt, Marilyn and Herb Comet, and Barbara Hansen.

Thanks, also, to the educators who read this book about the Internet as a way to become even better at what they do. Beginning to integrate technology into an already packed classroom and school agenda may seem impossible to others. But all we teachers know that for those who feel passionate about what they do, the difficult really is no problem, and the impossible just takes a little more time.

M. D. Roblyer
Carrollton, Georgia

ONE - *Understanding URLs*
How to Use Internet Addresses

New terms:

- *Uniform Resource Locator (URL)*
- *Server*
- *Domain name*
- *Domain designator*
- *Suffix*

Required Parts of a URL

Every home in the United States has an address so people can find it and make deliveries of mail and other items to it. Each place you "visit" on the Internet also has an address, and for much the same reasons. However, the Internet is less tolerant of mistakes in an address than is the U. S. Post Office! Each address must be entered exactly, with every punctuation mark in place, or it will not work.

Internet addresses are called Uniform Resource Locators, or **URLs**. Look at the example URL shown below in a browser window. The line where the URL is entered is called the address line:

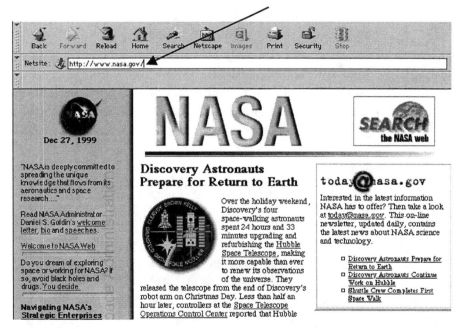

Try This! 1-1

http://www.prenhall. com/roblyer

Bring up the browser on your computer screen and enter this URL in the address line.
Then press Return or Enter to "travel" to this address on the Internet.

1

Every URL has four required parts (although it can have more optional ones that will be described later):

http://www.nasa.gov
    ❶   ❷   ❸ ❹

❶ Each web page address begins with **http://** which stands for HyperText Transfer Protocol. This shows it is an Internet address.

❷ Most, but not all, addresses contain **www,** which stands for World Wide Web.

A "server" is a computer that has a site on the Internet.

❸ The next part of the address here is **nasa**, the name of the computer or "server" to which you connect. Every server on the Internet has an assigned label called the "domain name." **nasa** shows that this computer belongs to the National Aeronautic and Space Administration, a government agency that offers educators a wealth of resources on its web site.

Domain designators for public schools always include the state name:

❹ Finally, another required part of the domain name, called a "domain designator," tells what kind of group owns the server. Some example domain designators are:

org = organization	**com** = business
gov = government agency	**edu** = university
k12.__.us = public schools	**net** = network
mil = military agency	**aus** = Australia

Examples:
k12.ny.us
(New York)

There are many more designators, and more are being added all the time as the need arises. The U. S. non-profit organization that sets up domain names is the Internet Corporation for Assigned Names and Numbers (ICANN).

k12.fl.us
(Florida)

You can learn more about ICANN at **http://www.icann.org**

Optional Parts of a URL

If an organization is a large one, it may have more than one server or it may split up a large computer into sections. Then the domain name will have more parts. For example, the University of Central Florida (**ucf**) has a server or section of a server called **itrc** owned by the Instructional Technology Resource Center:

http://www.itrc.ucf.edu

Optional parts called "suffixes" can come after a domain designator. Suffixes show locations on the server set aside for specific purposes. For example, the ITRC has a place to display an overview and summary of its activities. This is shown by the suffixes following the slashes:

http://www.itrc.ucf.edu/about/who.html

Try This! 1-2

http://www.prenhall. com/roblyer

Answer the following questions about the parts of the following URL in the spaces below.

http://www.kidlink.org/english/general/ index.html

- What does **www** stand for? _____

- What is the name of the computer or server that displays this site? _____

- Which part of the URL identifies this as an Internet address? _____

- What is the domain designator in this URL, and what kind of group does it show owns this site?

  _____

- Why are there slashes in this URL? _____

  _____

Three URL Uses

Three things to learn how to do with URLs are locate them, read them, and "fix" errors in them.

- **Locating URLs.** If you want to visit a site, but you don't know its URL, one way to find it is to make an educated guess. For example, let's say you want to find the website for the National Council of Social Studies. Since you know it will have an "org" designator and organizations usually use their initials in URLs, a good guess would be: **http://www.ncss.org**

Try This! 1-3

http://www.prenhall. com/roblyer

Guess a URL for each of the following. Then go on the Internet and type in the URLs to see if you are correct.

1. National Council of Teachers of Mathematics Correct answer p. 261:_____
2. The Music Educators National Conference: Correct answer p. 285:_____

All page numbers listed in this booklet refer to ***Integrating Educational Technology into Teaching, 2nd Edition.***

- **Reading URLs.** If someone gives you a URL, very often you can tell what and where it is by reading its parts. Look at an example from p. 273:

http://www.noaa.gov

If what you expected to get was a URL on weather, you might guess this is for the National Oceanic and Atmospheric Administration (NOAA), a government agency that offers students and teachers a wealth of up-to-date information on the weather.

Try This! 1-4

*http://www.prenhall.
com/roblyer*

*Can you read the URL for each of the following?
Go on the Internet, type in the URL, and go to the site to
see if you are correct.*

1. For gifted students: **http://www.nagc.org**
   Correct answer p. 315:_____
2. For a news network: **http://www.cnn.com**
   Correct answer p. 273:_____

• **Fixing errors in URLs.** Someone may give you a URL with an error in it (or you may write down a correct one incorrectly!). There are five common errors you can look for and correct:

Error #1–Omitting one of the parts. The most common omission is the "http://" or the "www."

Error #2–Wrong domain designator. People often substitute "com" for "org."

Error #3–Punctuation errors. People often confuse forward slashes (/) and back slashes (\), and hyphens (-) with underlines (_).

Error #4–Punctuation omitted. If you leave out a "dot" or a slash, the URL will not work.

Error #5–Misspellings. Most misspellings in URLs seem to occur in suffixes.

Try This! 1-5

http://www.prenhall. com/roblyer

Can you spot errors in each of the following URLs? Correct the error, then enter the URL in a browser to see if it works.

1. The Eisenhower National Clearinghouse, a site with lesson plans and other resources for teachers:

   What's the error? **http://enc.org**

   Correct answer p. 258: _____

2. The American School Heath Association:

   What's the error? **http://www.ashaweborg**

   Correct answer p. 305:_____

3. An organization with information about software publishing and copyright issues:

   What's the error? **http:\\www.spa.org**

   Correct answer p. 36:_____

4. An online store to buy technology resources

   What's the error? **http://www.cdw.edu**

   Correct answer p. 328:_____

TWO – *Navigating the Net*
How to Move Around in Web Pages

Five Ways to Go

New Terms

- *Hot links*
  or
  hot spots

You can move around from web page to web page on the Internet by using five different options. The first two options are to use two kinds of **links** that have been programmed into the web page itself. These are also known as "hot links" or "hot spots."

These links are programmed to send your browser to another location on the Internet, either within the site or to another site, when you click on them with your mouse. These programmed links can be:

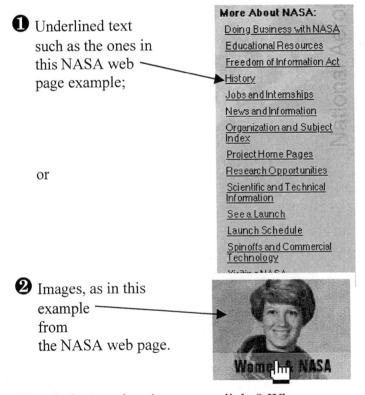

❶ Underlined text
such as the ones in
this NASA web
page example;

More About NASA:
Doing Business with NASA
Educational Resources
Freedom of Information Act
History
Jobs and Internships
News and Information
Organization and Subject Index
Project Home Pages
Research Opportunities
Scientific and Technical Information
See a Launch
Launch Schedule
Spinoffs and Commercial Technology

or

❷ Images, as in this
example
from
the NASA web page.

Women & NASA

How do know when images are links? When you pass a mouse pointer over the image (without clicking) and the pointer turns into a "browser hand" such as the one on the "Women & NASA" picture above, you know it is a link. Any part of a web page can be programmed to be a link.

Three other options are available on your browser menu bars. See the NASA web page example below.

❸ **Back button**

❹ **Forward button**

❺ **Go menu** (in *Internet Explorer*, use File Menu)

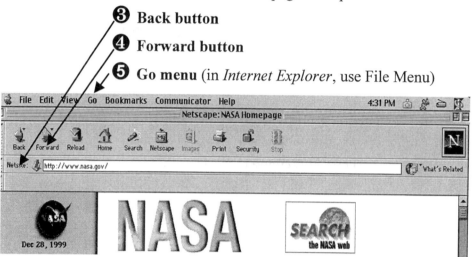

Forward and Back buttons let you go *one step at a time* on a linear path through a chain of web pages you have visited. For example, if you go to the NASA web page and click the "Education Resources" link (see below), you can click on the **Back button** to take you back to the NASA home page.

If you want to go back to the Education Resources page, use the **Forward button**.

You can travel back and forth in this way, just as if you were traveling back and forth visiting houses on the same road.

Notice that the **underlined links change color** after you click on them. Colors of visited and unvisited links depend on preferences specified in each browser.

More About NASA:

Doing Business with NASA

Educational Resources

Freedom of Information Act

History

Jobs and Internships

News and Information

Organization and Subject Index

Project Home Pages

Research Opportunities

Scientific and Technical Information

See a Launch

Launch Schedule

Spinoffs and Commercial Technology

Visiting NASA

Go to the NASA home page at:

http://www.nasa.gov

Do the following:

- Click on the "NASA for Kids" link.

- Pass your mouse pointer over the pictures on this page to locate one of the image links. Click on it.

- Click on the **Back button** twice to go back to the NASA home page.

- Click on the **Forward button** to go back though the pages you visited.

The Go Menu is only in Netscape. In Internet Explorer, past links are listed under the File Menu.

While the Forward and Back buttons let you go in a straight line, back and forth to pages you have been, the **Go menu** lets you "jump around" randomly to web pages you have visited. For example:

From the NASA home page we:

- Clicked on the Education Resources link
- Clicked on the listing of Education Programs
- Clicked on the Minority University Research and Education Division (MURAD)

The result is the Go menu listing you see below. You can click on the Go menu and scroll down to select and visit any of the pages listed there.

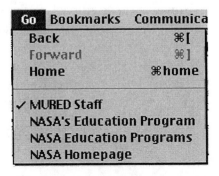

Try This! 2-2

http://www.prenhall.
com/roblyer

The
Smithsonian
has an "edu"
designator
because it is
considered a
higher
education
institution.

Try This! 2-3

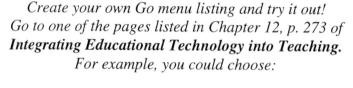

http://www.prenhall.
com/roblyer

Create your own Go menu listing and try it out!
Go to one of the pages listed in Chapter 12, p. 273 of
Integrating Educational Technology into Teaching.
For example, you could choose:

http://www.si.edu

This is the web site for the Smithsonian Institution.

Do the following:

• Click on some of the underlined and/or image links on this page. After each visit, look at the Go menu and see how it has changed.

• Now pull down the Go menu, select one of the pages listed there, and travel to it.

Try this final activity with Go menus:

Listings of pages you have visited will erase and a new list will start when you go "down another road." For example, after you visit the Smithsonian page, you go to some of the other pages listed on p. 273, in this order:

1 - The White House: **http://www.whitehouse.gov**
2 - Library of Congress: **http://lcweb.loc.gov**
3 - The History Channel: **http://historychannel.com**
4 - U. S. Census Bureau: **http://www.census.gov**

All these web pages above should be listed under "Go." However, now go back to the Library of Congress and go to *another* web site, let's say, the National Weather Service; check out the Go menu now. The History Channel and the U.S. Census Bureau (visits 3 and 4) will not be listed anymore! Go menus are programmed to act this way, so do not be surprised when pages you have visited are not listed in the menu.

THREE – *Starting Up Search Engines*
How to Locate Information on the Internet

What Is a Search Engine?

In many ways, the Internet is a reflection of our world: a place rich in resources and information. But before the Internet, it was much more difficult to locate specific resources or items of information in our world. Now there is so much information on the Internet that companies have developed special searching programs to help us locate things.

These searching programs are called **search engines**. There are two different kinds of search engines:

Search engines are sometimes called "web crawlers."

❶ **Regular search engines.** The most popular are:

* Alta Vista   http://altavista.digital.com
* Excite   http://www.excite.com
* InfoSeek   http://www.infoseek.com
* Magellan   http://www.mckinley.com
* Yahoo!   http://www.yahoo.com

❷ **Meta-search engines.** These are programs that use more than one other search engine at the same time to locate things. Examples:

* **Ask Jeeves**   http://www.askjeeves.com
* **Dog Pile**   http://www.dogpile.com
* **Metacrawler**   http://www.metacrawler.com
* **Mamma.com**   http://mamma.com

Two Way to Use a Search Engine

Both types of search engines can be used in two basic ways:
* **Subject index searches.** The search engine site provides a list of topics you can click on.

* **Keywords.** Type in combinations of words you think could be found in the URLs of sites or documents you want.

Try This! 3-1

*http://www.prenhall.
com/roblyer*

To examine these ways, try these examples. First:

Go to the Yahoo! search engine at:

http://www.yahoo.com

Example #1: Using subject index searches. Let's say that after reading about distance programs in Chapter 7, you are wondering how many distance learning programs there are in K-12 schools. If you used "distance learning" keywords, you would get a great many higher education sites. So you might want to begin with a subject search under Education, K-12.

All the underlined text titles you see on Yahoo!'s main page actually are hot links of categories you can click on to locate Internet web sites under that heading.

The listed results of an Internet search are sometimes called "hits."

• Find and click on the link that says "Education." The search engine sends you to yet another listing.

• Find and click on the link for "K-12." It sends you to yet another listing. Click on "Distance learning," and you see a great many links related to distance programs in K-12 schools. Each link is a web page.

Try This! 3-2

*http://www.prenhall.
com/roblyer*

Example #2: Using keywords. If you know certain words would be in the titles of web sites you are looking for, you may want to do a keyword search. Let's say you are intrigued by what you read about voice recognition on page 232 in *Integrating Educational Technology into Teaching's* Chapter 9. Try the following to locate more information:

• Find the box on the Yahoo! site that looks like the one below and type the words voice AND recognition (joined by the word AND).

| | Search |

- You also can type in phrases to do a search. For example, try "voice recognition" using quote marks around the phrase. Either way, you get a listing of companies and organizations that are doing things with this technology.

Many sites have their own built-in search engine that lets you use keywords to search the contents of the site. Look for the phrase "Search this site."

Each search engine site has its own "syntax" for joining keywords in various ways. One search engine might use AND to connect the keywords:

Example: software AND evaluation

while another search engine uses plus signs:

Example: + software + evaluation

The University of Central Florida's Instructional Technology Resource Center (ITRC) has a very useful summary of when and how to use each of these search engines. Look for it at:

http://www.itrc.ucf.edu/conferences/pres/ srchtool.html

Which Search Engine Should I Use?

Also, different search engines are useful for different purposes. Examples taken from the ITRC site include:

- **To browse a broad topic:**
  Use Yahoo! or Magellan

- **To search for a narrow topic:**
  Alta Vista, Excite, or Infoseek

- **To search the largest Internet amount:**
  Metacrawler or Ask Jeeves (meta-search engines)

- **To search only reviewed sites:**
  Magellan

- **To search for educational materials or reviews:**
  U. S. DOE website: http://ed.gov/free/

Try This! 3-3

http://www.prenhall.
com/roblyer

Try your hand at doing some searches to locate additional information on the subjects covered in Chapters 10-14 of your book. For a complete listing of search engines and their uses, see

http://www.searchenginewatch.com

Chapter 10: Technology in Language Arts and Foreign Language Instruction – Page 246 gives KidPub (http://www.launchsite.org), a web site that publishes children's writing and helps kids connect with other young writers. Can you locate other web sites that support young writers?

Chapter 11: Technology in Science and Mathematics Instruction – Page 260 describes instructional uses of graphing calculators. Can you locate some lesson plans that focus on graphing calculators?

Chapter 12: Technology in Social Studies Instruction – Page 273 gives a site for the History Channel. Can you locate other sites that could give your students information on the U. S. Civil War?

Chapter 13: Technology in Music and Art Instruction – Page 283 gives several web sites to let students see example of various works of art. Can you locate 5 art museums where your students could go on "virtual field trips"?

Chapter 14: Technology in Physical Education and Health – Page 298 gives a web site of drug-related street terms and other drug information. Can you locate other web sites that might help teach drug prevention?

Chapter 15: Technology in Special Education – Page 308 describes some of the recent legislation dealing with education of special needs students. Can you locate any more recent federal legislation on this topic?

FOUR – *Using Bookmarks*
How to Mark Web Pages for Later Use

How to Make a Bookmark

New Terms

• *Bookmark*

You may visit so many sites on the Internet that you quickly can lose track of where you found a valuable site on a certain topic. You could write all of them down, but a quicker way is to use bookmarks.

Bookmarks is a feature in your browser. It lets you mark the address of sites you want to remember. Making a bookmark is very simple. Just travel to the site, then go to the Bookmark menu and select "Add Bookmark." A bookmark title for that site appears at the bottom of the bookmark list. See the example below for adding the Global Schoolhouse site:

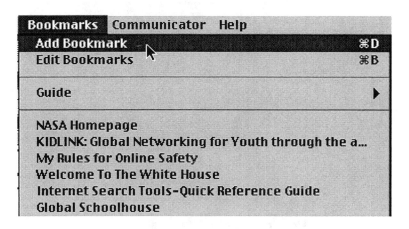

Try This! 4-1

http://www.prenhall.
com/roblyer

Try making a bookmark.
A site you will want to remember is the one for the
International Society for Technology in Education (ISTE),
described on pp. 7 and 15 of the textbook.

http://www.iste.org

Go to this site on the Internet
and create a bookmark for it.

How to Delete Bookmarks

You may want to mark some sites only temporarily, then delete them. On many browser versions, the edit feature is listed on the Bookmark menu (see p. 15). Other browser versions may list it under the Edit menu.

To delete a bookmark, select Edit Bookmarks. A window will appear with a list of your current bookmarks. Click on the bookmark you want to delete and select "Cut" or "Clear" from the Edit menu, as shown below:

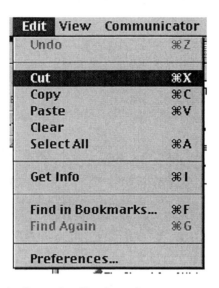

How to Organize Bookmarks

As noted on p. 217 of *Integrating Educational Technology into Teaching*, "well-prepared bookmark files are great resources for teachers and should be shared with others who have similar interests." But what is a "well-prepared bookmark file?"

In order for a bookmark collection to be most useful to you and others, it should be organized into sections, much like a library or any collection of materials. After you create bookmarks, you can organize them into categories of related items.

For example, let's say you make bookmarks for each of the Language Arts Instruction sites listed and described on p. 245:

National Council of Teachers of English
http://www.ncte.org

Teachers and Writers Collaborative
http://www.twc.org/

Word Play
http://www.wolinskyweb.com/word.htm

Rensselaer Writing Center
http://www.rpi.edu/web/writingcenter/

Then, create other bookmarks for sites such as:

The Kidreach Online Reading Center
http://www.westga.edu/~kidreach/

> National Council of Teachers of English
> Welcome To Teachers & Writers OnLine
> Word Play
> The KidReach Reading Center
> Writing Center

Now you want to place these into a section of your bookmarks file and add other bookmarks on this topic later. Here is what you do:

Bring up the Edit Bookmarks option in your browser. Create a new folder by selecting "New" under the File menu:

Give the folder an appropriate name: for example, "English Teaching sites." Now drag the icons for all four sites, one at a time, into the folder you just created. See below for an example of what this might look like in the Bookmark menu after a folder is created in this way:

Bookmarks	Communicator	Help	
Add Bookmark			⌘D
Edit Bookmarks			⌘B
Guide			▶
English teaching sites			

National Council of Teachers of English
Welcome To Teachers & Writers OnLine
Word Play
The KidReach Reading Center
Writing Center

Try This! 4-2

http://www.prenhall. com/roblyer

Try creating and organizing your own bookmark files. Create bookmarks for some or all of the content area chapters in the book. Look on the following pages to get you started:

pp. 245-246:   Chapter 10–Language Arts

p. 249:   Chapter 10–Foreign Languages

p. 258:   Chapter 11–Science

p. 261:   Chapter 11–Mathematics

p. 273:   Chapter 12– Social Studies

p. 283:   Chapter 13–Art

pp. 285-286   Chapter 13–Music

pp. 297-298   Chapter 14–Physical Ed. & Health

p. 315, p. 321   Chapter 15–Special Education

If you find errors in the URLs, try correcting them using the strategies listed on page 5 of this book.

After you create the bookmarks, create a folder for each topic and drag in the bookmarks related to it.

FIVE – *Evaluating Internet Information*
How to Assess Web Site Quality

Why You Should be Careful

• *Web page criteria*

• *Site map*

At a time when everything in the world seems so high-tech and highly controlled, the Internet is, in some ways, a wild frontier. While there are oversight agencies that set up and monitor general items such domain designators (see p. 2 of this book), no one controls who posts web pages or the quality of their content.

Three kinds of problems arise from this lack of control. One of these, the hazards of offensive or dangerous subject matter or illegal activities, is dealt with in the next section (**SIX – Avoiding Internet Pitfalls**). The other two problems are less perilous but still have serious implications for teachers and students. Web pages can be less than useful for two reasons:

- **Content.** The Internet's vast storehouse of information, unfortunately, contains some that is incomplete, inaccurate, and/or out of date, and even some sites that are works of complete fiction present themselves as fact.

- **Design.** We have learned a great deal in recent years about what makes a web site functional and easy to use. However, some sites are so poorly designed that people may find it difficult or impossible to locate and/or read information they have to offer.

Page 216 of *Integrating Educational Technology into Teaching* gives a summary of criteria gleaned from several sources for evaluating web site quality, usefulness, and reliability. These criteria are described here in more depth in terms of the two general qualities listed above.

Criteria for Evaluating Web Page Content

Students frequently accept as authoritative any information they find on the Internet. However, young people must learn that blind acceptance of any information (on the Internet or elsewhere!) is a risky practice. An essential skill for the Information Age is being able to evaluate information critically and look for these signs that content is accurate and reliable:

- **Known author.** The web page author is a person or organization with a recognized name and authority. Be wary of those in which the author is not stated, whose credibility would be difficult to ascertain, or who have a known bias.

- **Contact information.** Authors of genuine sites usually give an e-mail address and/or other information one may use to contact them and ask questions about the content.

- **Frequent updates.** The site should list the last time the site was updated on the front page. Information has more credibility if the site is well maintained.

- **References or links to other sites.** Some sites list documents they used as sources for the information. Others contain links to other sites one may use to verify statements and facts. Any information on a web page should be able to be verified by other sources.

Teachers can help students understand how important it is to confirm web site information by doing an activity such as the following one.

Try This! 5-1

http://www.prenhall. com/roblyer

Look at the following site. (HINT: There is no such place as New Hartford, MN!) Apply criteria for assessing information accuracy. http://www.lme.mankato.msus.edu/newhartford/ newhtfd.html

Other links to "spurious web sites" may be found at:

http://www.users.csbsju.edu/
%7Eproske/evalwebp.html

Criteria for Evaluating Web Page Design

Another way to help verify the quality and accuracy of information on a web page is to look at its design. Web pages have more credibility if they are easy to use and have a professional-looking layout. Look for these characteristics to judge design quality:

• **Good structure and organization.** The first page of the site indicates clearly how to get to its various parts. Some sites do this with an option bar that appears at the top, bottom, or side of every page in the site. That way you can get easily to any part. See this example option bar from the U. S. Department of Education at: http://www.ed.gov/

Text or graphic links are clear. Branches are organized so that you can get back to the main page in no more than three clicks. One device for large sites provides a link to a **site map** or an at-a-glance guide to the contents. See the example below from the State University of West Georgia at http://www.westga.edu:

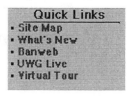

• **Visual design.** Pages are designed for good readability. There are a limited number of colors and fonts; fonts are easy to read, and colors are selected for contrast with the background. Graphics do not distract from reading the content. You can tell from looking at an icon what information you will get by clicking on it.

• **Easy navigation.** Pages load quickly. It's easy to get around in the site. Links are provided so you can get back to the main page from any part of the site. The most important information is given at the top of the page. All links work as they should. Larger sites have their own built-in search engine. See the example search engine below at the U. S. House of Representatives web site at:
http://thomas.loc.gov/

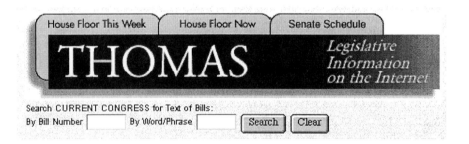

• **Miscellaneous.** Pages are short enough that each can be printed quickly. Video, sounds, and graphics help present the information, but the page provides alternate ways of getting the same information for those who lack advanced browser capabilities.

Try This! 5-2

http://www.prenhall. com/roblyer

Evaluate the web page for your own organization according to the qualities described above.

What improvements could you suggest?

More Information on Evaluating Web Pages

Additional information and links to web page evaluation criteria checklists and rubrics may be found at the following sites:

Evaluating Internet Resources – A summary of general criteria for evaluating web page quality from the Binghamton University Library:

http://library.lib.binghamton.edu/search/evaluation.html

Ten C's for Evaluating Internet Sources – Ten categories of criteria for evaluating quality and reliability of information on an Internet site developed by the University of Wisconsin–Eau Claire Library:

http://www.uwec.edu/Admin/Library/Guides/tencs.html

Web Evaluation for Primary, Middle, and Secondary Grades –Three checklists of criteria K–12 students can use to evaluate the quality of web sites.

http://www.siec.k12.in.us/~west/online/eval.htm

Web Page Evaluation Criteria and Tips
(from p. 216 of *Integrating Educational Technology into Teaching*, 2nd edition)

1.   **Content**
_____ All information is accurate. The "last time updated" date is given.
_____ Information is complete but not excessive or redundant.
_____ Information is well organized and clearly labeled.
_____ Information is interesting, informative, and worthwhile.
_____ Information is not redundant to other sources; there is a reason to put it on the Web.
_____ All text has correct spelling, grammar, and punctuation.
_____ Level of content and vocabulary is appropriate for intended audience.
_____ Content is free from stereotyping, coarse or vulgar language, or matter that could be offensive to typical users.
_____ Author(s) of the page are clearly identified.
_____ The page gives an e-mail address or other way to contact author(s).

2.   **Visual and Audio Design**
_____ The site has a consistent, common look and feel across pages.
_____ Graphics, animations, videos, and sounds make an important contribution.
_____ Pages have only one or two fonts.
_____ Each page uses a limited numbers of colors, especially for text.
_____ Colors have been selected to be compatible with the *Netscape* 216-color palette.
_____ Type colors/styles and text-to-background contrast were selected for readability.
_____ Each graphic is designed to fit 640 x 480 pixel screens (allowing for scroll bars/toolbars).
_____ Each page is limited to 2-3 screens; the most important information is at the top.
_____ The pages are simply and attractively designed and make a user want to read them.

3.   **Navigation**
_____ Pages load quickly.
_____ Pages have a simple, consistent navigation scheme for quick, easy navigation.
_____ The first page shows clearly how the site is organized and how to get to all items.
_____ Text and icon links are easy to identify. Graphics and sounds are clearly identified.
_____ Icons have been well chosen to represent the information they link to.
_____ Each supporting page has a link back to the home page.

4.   **Miscellaneous (for larger sites and pages)**
_____ Requests for private information are secure.
_____ Page information is kept short enough that it can be printed out quickly.
_____ Users can choose to load alternate versions of pages (e.g., text only, smaller images).
_____ The site has its own search engine for locating things within the pages.
_____ Branching is organized so all content is three clicks or fewer from the home page.

Use the following tips to make your sites and pages easier to design and use:

_____ Organize the site on paper ahead of time before inputting it to the computer.
_____ To speed loading, limit graphics to no more than 50K and re-use images whenever possible.
_____ Use GIFs for line art or graphics with limited colors and sharp edges; use JPEGs for photos with many colors and smooth gradients. Avoid PICT and other formats that must be converted by users.
_____ Test your page in a real browser.
_____ Use a GIF spacer (1x1 transparent GIF) to space paragraphs, indents, or alignments on pages.

SIX – *Avoiding Internet Pitfalls*
How to Recognize and Prevent Problems

Types of Problems

New Terms

• *Firewalls*

• *Filtering software*

As has been noted before, the Internet is a reflection of our society. This means that, like the world at large, there are some places on the Internet that pose potential dangers for those who venture out on its paths. This does not mean people should avoid taking advantage of the Internet altogether, anymore than we should refrain from traveling because of the potential dangers of accidents or other threats. It does mean that educators and their students should be aware of the kinds of problems that can arise when they use the Internet and take steps to prevent them.

Pages 218-219 of *Integrating Educational Technology into Teaching* outline several of these potential pitfalls. These issues are discussed here with an emphasis on things educators can do to make the Internet a safer, more worry-free place for teaching and learning.

Methods to address five kinds of Internet problem areas are described here:

• #1: How to keep students from going to sites with inappropriate materials

• #2: Putting in place safeguards against people who use the Internet to take advantage of others

• #3: How to protect your financial transactions on the Internet

• #4: Protecting against viruses (see page 40 of the textbook for additional information on viruses)

• #5: How to make sure you observe copyright law when using Internet resources

Problem #1: Blocking Access to Sites with Inappropriate Materials

Like a big-city bookstore, the Internet has materials that parents and teachers may not want students to see, either because they are inappropriate for an age level or because they contain information or images considered objectionable. Unfortunately, it is easy to access these sites unintentionally. For example, only three letters (the domain designator) differentiate the web site for our nation's Executive Branch (http://www.whitehouse.gov/) from one with X-rated images and materials.

Since it is so easy to access these sites without meaning to, classroom or lab Internet usage rules are no safeguard against this problem. Most schools have found that the best way to prevent access to sites with inappropriate materials is to install **firewall** and/or **filtering software**.

- **Filtering software.** An individual or a school can purchase and install these programs on one or more computers. Munro (1998) reviewed some of these programs (see *IETT* p. 218). Although there are more on the market, some of the ones she recommended include:

  Cyber Patrol (http://www.learningco.com)
  Cyber Sentinel (http://www.securitysoft.com/)
  Cybersnoop (http://www.pearlsw.com)
  Cybersitter (http://www.cybersitter.com)
  Net Nanny (http://www.netnanny.com)
  Surf Watch (http://www1.surfwatch.com)
  WatchDog (http://www.sarna.net/watchdog)
  WebChaperone (http://www.webchaperone.com/)
  X-Stop (http://www.xstop.com)

Filtering programs also have other desirable features, such as keeping track of the time students spend on Internet sessions and reports of attempted site accesses.

- **Firewall software.** Unlike filtering programs that can be bought and installed on individual computers, these programs are part of the server's network operating system, the software that makes the network function. Firewalls usually are installed at the district level, since most schools are part of a larger network.

Both filtering programs and firewalls block access to sites either on the basis of keywords, a list of off-limits sites, or a combination of these methods.

Try This! 6-1

http://www.prenhall. com/roblyer

The reference to the full article by Munro is listed on p. 227 of the textbook. Review Munro's article in summary form online at:

http://www.zdnet.com/pcmag/stories/reviews/ 0,6755,283666,00.html

Note that you can do searches for articles on this and other related topics in several magazines using the ZDNet search engine at this site.

Problem #2: Protecting Students Against Online Problems

Because they lack the experience that helps alert them to dangerous situations, young people are at special risk on the Internet in two different ways:

- **Online predators.** Young people tend to believe what they hear and read. Therefore, in a chatroom they may not consider that a 12-year-old named "Mary" may actually be a 50-year-old man.

- **Sales pitches aimed at children.** This is a problem similar to that posed by television commercials. Many Internet sites have colorful, compelling images that encourage people to buy. Young people may make commitments they cannot fulfill.

One very helpful Internet site that addresses these issues is:

http://www.safekids.com/child_safety.htm

It has a document called *Safety on the Information Highway*, which was developed for the National Center for Missing and Exploited Children by newspaper columnist Lawrence J. Magid.

Kids' Rules for Online Safety

Magid says, "Teenagers are particularly at risk because they often use the computer unsupervised and because they are more likely than younger children to participate in online discussions regarding companionship, relationships, or sexual activity."

He recommends teaching children a set of online rules. See the list of these rules at:

http://www.safekids.com/kidsrules.htm

Try This! 6-2

http://www.prenhall. com/roblyer

Think about some ways you could teach these online rules to students.

For example, you might have students create a multimedia presentation of the rules listed above.

(See IETT pp. 180-181 for guidelines on doing student-created multimedia products.)

Problem #3: Avoiding Fraud on the Internet

Teachers may find that the fastest, easiest way to order computer products and/or teaching materials is to go to a company's web site and order them online. However, most areas of the Internet are not secure. That is, what you do on the Internet can be monitored by others. Some people use this monitoring capability to look for a credit card number or other information they can use fraudulently.

As online consumers, teachers must be sure to purchase products only from well-known, reputable sites that offer a secure server. Secure servers have special programs to prevent outside monitoring of transactions. The URL for a secure server usually begins with "https" instead of the usual "http."

Problem #4: Protecting Your Computer from Online Viruses

As described on pages 40 and 219 of your textbook, viruses are programs written for malicious purposes. Two ways to get viruses on your computer from the Internet are by:

- **E-mail attachments with viruses.** An increasingly popular way to send files and programs to friends or colleagues is to attach them to e-mail messages. However, if a computer contains a virus that is programmed to attach itself to files, the virus can be sent inadvertently along with the file. When the person receiving the attachment opens it, the virus transfers to his/her computer.

- **Downloaded files and programs with viruses.** Procedures for transferring or downloading programs, documents, and other items from an Internet site to a computer are described in **Section Eight** of this book. As with e-mail attachments, viruses can attach themselves to files and programs and be received along with the item being downloaded.

What can you do to prevent these problems? Three procedures are recommended:

- **Keep virus protection software up to date.** Always maintain and use a copy of a program designed to detect and safeguard against viruses.

   (See a list of some of these virus protection programs on p. 328 of the textbook.)

- **Download only from reputable sites.** If you have never heard of or dealt with an organization before, downloading files from them can be risky. Shareware programs are a frequent source of attached viruses.

- **Do not open e-mail attachments from unknown sources.** Some viruses are programmed to send e-mails and attachments automatically and to infect the computers that open them. Be wary of e-mails from people or organizations you don't know. Do not open a suspicious e-mail or attachment before you confirm it has been sent for legitimate purposes.

Problem #5: Copyright Issues for Educators

The Internet is such a rich and easy-to-access source of documents, images, and other resources, it sometimes is easy to forget that many of these resources are copyrighted and protected by U. S. copyright laws.

To prevent problems, teach your students to look for copyright notices at the sites whose items you want to use. Then do the following:

- **If the site clearly is copyrighted**, contact the owners to request permission to use items.

- **If the site has no copyright statement,** be sure to reference the site by its URL and owner name on any materials you create with the resources.

SEVEN – *Downloading and Using Images*
How to Obtain and Use Internet Graphics

New Terms

• *Download*
• *Image formats*
• *gif*
• *jpeg*

Why Images Are Important

The Internet has been around in text format since 1969. However, it became the society-wide phenomenon we know today only when the first web browser, *Mosaic*, made it possible for the Internet to appear on computer screens as images.

Why do images make such a difference? There may be two reasons. First, pictures are an "information shortcut." The old adage that "a picture is worth a thousand words" means that people grasp many concepts more quickly when they are presented as images rather than as text. Second, people seem able to remember a great deal of information visually.

But it is possible to take advantage of the visual tapestry of the Internet in ways other than receiving information. You can use your browser to "capture" or download any image you see from any web page and store it on your computer. Once you download an image, you can use it in a word processing or desktop publishing file, or even to create your own web pages.

How to Download Images

Let's say you wanted to have students use word processing to make an illustrated booklet of the three branches of the U. S. government. You might go to sites for each of these branches and capture images for them to use in their booklets.

Look at the following example. Three images (the two flags and the image of the White House) appear on the White House web site at:

http://www.whitehouse.gov

See a picture of this web site on the following page.

You can capture or download the image of the White House from this site. To "grab" an image from a web page is very simple, but the procedure differs slightly between Macintosh and Windows computers. To download the White House image, do the following:

Try This! 7-1

http://www.prenhall. com/roblyer

Downloading images in this way is a feature provided in your browser software.

• **On a Macintosh:** Click on the White House image but, instead of letting up the mouse after you click, hold it down until a menu like this one appears:

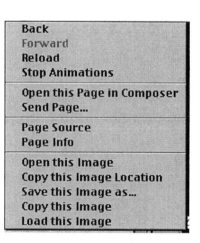

Now drag down and select the "Save this image as..." option to save the image to your computer. See directions for what to do next after the Windows PC step.

- **On a Windows PC**. Right-click on the White House image and, instead of letting up the mouse after you click, hold it down until a menu appears:

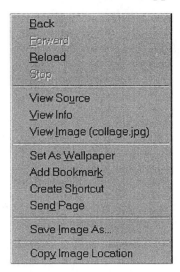

Now drag down and select the "Save image as..." option to save the image to your computer.

After you select the "Save as" option, a box will appear to allow you to save the image on your computer. Depending on whether you have a Macintosh or PC computer, this box will look something like the following:

The file name that will appear here will always be the name under which it was stored when it was put on the web page. The file name under which this White House image was stored is "bevel.jpg."

However, before you click "Save" to save the file, you can change this name to something you may find easier to remember. For example:

Images on U. S. government web sites usually are considered public domain and may be used without permission for educational purposes.

Downloading an image from the Internet is easy. But remember that many images you find on web pages are copyrighted, and their legal use is determined by copyright law and the owner of the web site. If you are not sure if you can use an image legally, contact the web site owner to request permission.

What to Do with Downloaded Images

After you save an image on your computer, you can insert it in documents or other web pages. However, you may need to change the **image format** from the original file format to another one.

Several image formats have been developed over the years to serve various purposes; either a certain computer or operating system required it, or certain formats deal better with differences among image types (e.g., photos rather than drawn images or clip art).

You can tell the format of an image by its suffix. For example, the White House image was a **jpeg** file format. Images downloaded from web pages will be in one of the following formats:

- **gif** – Stands for "Graphics Interchange Format." Used for drawn images, illustrations, or clip art.

- **jpeg** – Stands for "Joint Photographic Experts Group." Used for photographs.

The user manual of each software package tells which image format it can take.

If you want to use images to do your own web pages (see *IETT* pp. 215-216), they must be in one of these two formats.

However, if you want to use images from the web in other software packages such as presentation software (see *IETT* pp. 150-152) or desktop publishing (see *IETT* pp. 142-143), you may have to obtain and use an image manipulation software such as *Adobe PhotoShop* to save the image into another format.

There are several other types of image formats. Here are some of the more common ones:

- **bmp** – Stands for "bitmapped." A standard format developed originally for use on DOS and Windows-compatible computers.

- **eps** – Stands for "Encapsulated Post Script." Developed to transfer artwork between any software packages that used PostScript printing files.

- **pdf** – Stands for "Portable Document Format." Used to store document pages as images. (See **Section Eight** of this booklet for more information on pdf files and software to read them.)

- **pict** – Short for "Picture" format, this format was developed originally for use on Macintosh computers.

- **tif** – Stands for "Tagged Image File." Designed to be a flexible format for exchanging files among various software application and computers.

Two kinds of programs in which you will want to use images are described in *IETT* Chapter 5:
presentation software (pp. 150-152)
(e. g., PowerPoint)
and **word processing software** (pp. 142-143)
(e. g., PageMaker).

Now practice using images in these kinds of packages:

Try This! 7-2

http://www.prenhall.com/roblyer

Let's say you want to do a *PowerPoint* presentation for your school or district. Go to your school web site and download its logo to your computer. Now insert that image on the title page of a *PowerPoint* presentation. Here is an example of how it might look:

Carrollton City Schools

A presentation for the Carrollton PTA
Fall, 2001

Try This! 7-3

http://www.prenhall. com/roblyer

Page 125 of *IETT* has a lesson plan on "Exploring Political Parties." Obtain images from web pages such as the following and use them in your word processing program to create an overview handout of the parties:

- **Democratic National Committee web site**
  http://www.democrats.org/index.html

- **Republican National Committee web site**
  http://www.rnc.org/

- **Reform Party web site**
  http://www.reformparty.org/

Kinds of Resources to be Downloaded

New Terms

- *Plug-in*
- *PDF document*
- *Streaming video*
- *Streaming audio*

Web browsers made the Internet visual, but recent developments have given it sound and motion. Special programs called **plug-ins** have been created to allow people to see and hear these multimedia features that make the Internet increasingly life-like.

Although plug-ins tend to change and update rapidly, the Internet has a built-in way of allowing people to take full advantage of the Internet's multimedia features and keep up with advancements required to use them. Instead of buying the programs on disks, Internet users can download many of them directly from the company site. Some of the kinds of programs you will need and procedures for downloading them are described in this section.

Programs and Plug-ins You Will Need

- **Updated browser versions.** Most new computers come with a browser program stored on the hard drive. However, browsers change versions frequently, and it is necessary to keep an up-to-date version in order to see newer Internet features. Download newer versions of browsers from the Netscape and Microsoft web sites:

Netscape Communicator® is available at:
http://www.netscape.com/

Internet Explorer® is available at:
http://www.microsoft.com/downloads/

- **Adobe *Acrobat*® viewer plug-in.** This program lets you see **PDF** (Portable Document Format) files. These are pages stored as images so they may printed out with a page appearance identical to the original document. PDFs are particularly important when the original text contains both print and images, or when one wants to see the appearance of the original document. For example, one might photograph and store the pages of the Declaration of Independence so history students could see them. Although the program to create PDF files must be purchased, the *Acrobat*® viewer plug-in required to see already-stored PDF files is available free from Adobe, Inc at:

**http://www.adobe.com/products/
acrobat/readstep.html**

- **Streaming video and audio player plug-ins.** A new and exciting Internet capability is seeing action or hearing sounds live on the Internet, as they happen. Streaming is so called because it sends or "streams" images and sounds a little at a time so one need not download the files completely before using the contents. However, once these files are seen and stored on a computer, they also may be seen and/or heard later. *RealPlayer*® and *Real Jukebox*® are examples of these plug-ins.

Real Player® and *Real Jukebox*® are available at:

Real Networks.com
http://www.real.com/

- **Movie player plug-in.** Videos that have been digitized and stored as movie files may be viewed through a plug-in. One of the earliest, but still most useful, plug-ins for seeing these videos is the *QuickTime®* player available from the Apple Company. Although originally designed as a movie player, more recent versions of *QuickTime®* also can be used with streaming video and audio.

The *QuickTime®* player is available from:

Apple Computer, Inc.
http://www.apple.com/

How to Download Browsers and Other Programs

Downloading a program or plug-in is easy; simply go to the web site and follow the directions! Usually, the site provides very clear steps. Once you supply the information the site requests and click on the button to begin downloading, you will see a box similar to the following:

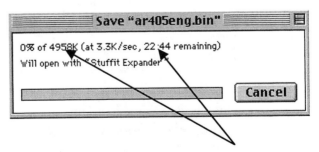

This box shows you how the download is progressing and appropriately how much time is left before the download is complete.

Since installing plug-ins can be tricky, computer novices may need help the first time.

The downloading process usually places an icon for the program on your desktop. After the plug-in is downloaded, you will have to double-click on this icon to install the plug-in in the appropriate folder or directory. The program itself provides directions.

There are many more plug-ins than the ones described here; you will see them as you use various Internet sites. The procedure for downloading them is basically the same for all of them.

Try This! 8-1

http://www.prenhall. com/roblyer

Download the four plug-ins described in this section to your own computer.
Try each of them out with the files indicated.

❶ *Adobe Acrobat®:* **http://www.adobe.com/ products/acrobat/ readstep.html**

Now use this plug-in to look at the PDF versions of U. S. DOE reports such as *The Corporate Imperative: A Business Guide for Implementing Strategic Education Partnerships* available at:
http://www.ed.gov/pubs/strategicpartner/

❷ *RealPlayer®:* **http://www.real.com/**
and
❸ *RealJukebox®*

Now use these plug-ins to look at the multimedia site on The Digital Divide available at:
http://www.digitaldivide.org/

❹ *QuickTime®:* **http://www.apple.com/**

Now use this plug-in to look at *QuickTime®* movies created by K-12 students available at:
http://www.apple.com/education/k12/products/dv/

NINE – *Internet Troubleshooting*
How to Recognize and Address
Common Errors

New Terms

• *Dead link*
• *HTML*
• *Java*
• *Perl*

Three Kinds of Errors

Like most technologies, the Internet presents its share of "head scratchers." The majority of these errors and problems can be corrected easily; others require more complicated "fixes" or adjustments. Three of the most common difficulties for Internet users are:

- **Site connection failures.** After you enter the URL, the site won't come up on the screen.

- **Site features won't work.** The animation, movie, or sound file on the site will not work.

- **Memory errors.** The computer or the browser does not have enough Random Access Memory (RAM) to load a site or use a plug-in.

Problem ❶: A Site Won't Connect

This is the most common problem people encounter, and it may occur for any of several reasons. Each problem has an error message that indicates the cause.

- **URL syntax errors.** As mentioned in Section One of this book, each dot and letter in a URL has to be correct, or the site won't load. The most common error message for this problem looks like this:

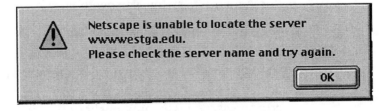

If this message appears, check the URL syntax and make sure you have not:

-Confused the letter "l" with the number "1"
-Confused the letter "O" with the number "0"
-Confused the hyphen "-" with the underline "_"
-Confused the forward slash "/" with the backward slash "\"
-Omitted a required punctuation mark
-Misspelled a part of the URL
-Used the wrong domain designator (e.g., "edu" instead of "org")

Many URL errors occur in suffixes that follow the domain designator. You can try omitting all suffixes beyond the slash and going directly to the main part of the URL. Sometimes the main page shows links, or the site has a built-in search engine you can use to locate the page you want.

- **Local or domain server down.** If you have checked the URL syntax and are positive it is correct, it may be that the server that hosts the web site is not working temporarily. It may have a technical problem or simply may be down for regular maintenance. In this case, you may get an error message like the one shown previously. You can wait for a day or two and try it again.

  A more rare cause of connection failures is that the server handling Internet traffic for the network or for users in the geographic region is not working properly. The error message usually says "Failure to resolve domain error. Try this site again later."

- **Bad or dead links.** If the URL repeatedly fails to connect and you are positive the syntax is correct, the site may have been taken off the Internet. This is a **bad** or **dead link**. If this is the case, you may get the same error message given previously or the site may provide a message that says "bad link."

- **Firewalls.** Sometimes a site will not connect because a network's firewall blocks it. (See **Section Six** of this book.) If you think your network's firewall is blocking your access to a site in error, contact your network administrator and request that this be adjusted.

Problem ❷: Internet Features Won't Work

If an Internet site indicates that it has a special feature such as an animation, movie, or sound but it will not work for you, there are three possible causes:

- **Plug-in required.** It may be that your computer does not have the special program or plug-in required to see the movie or sound. Usually, if a special plug-in is needed, the site will have a link to where you can go to download the plug-in and install it on your computer. (See **Section Eight** on Downloading Programs and Plug-ins.)

- **Compatibility errors.** The Internet works because there are agreements in place about how to make various machines and programs "talk" to each other. However, sometimes there are differences between operating systems or versions of software that make them incompatible. Some sites can be seen only with *Netscape*; some only with *Internet Explorer*. The web page usually indicates if it requires a specific browser.

- **Programming errors.** As described on page 213 of *IETT*, Internet web pages usually are written in a combination of three programming languages: HyperText Markup Language (HTML), Java, and less often, Perl. HTML is the basic language that sets up and formats a page, Java is used for graphics and animation, and Perl is used to write "CGI scripts," which are used when the site wants people to enter information into the web page (e.g., a survey).

If you get a Javascript error message, try updating your browser version. (See **Section Eight** on Downloading Programs and Plug-ins.) If you have an up-to-date browser version but still get a Javascript error message, it may be that there really is an error in the Java or Perl language of the program or script. In this case, the only thing you can do is to contact the site and alert them to the error.

Try This! 9-1

*http://www.prenhall.
com/roblyer*

Look at the HTML code for a web page on your screen by selecting "Source Code" from the View menu in your browser.

Problem ❸: Out-of-Memory Error Messages Appear

In addition to the problems described above, you may get errors because your computer or the program lacks the memory required to see the images at the site or to run the plug-in. On a Macintosh, you may get an error message that says you have insufficient memory or the site may keep trying to load indefinitely.

If this occurs, try allocating more memory to the browser. Click once on the icon for the browser and select "Get Info" from the file menu. When the box shown here appears, enter larger numbers in the boxes.

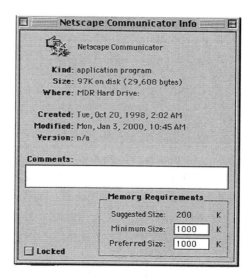

TEN – *Integrating the Internet into Teaching Strategies, Resources, and Lesson Links*

Powerful Teaching and Learning Strategies

Now that you have learned skills you need to be a skilled Internet traveler, you can begin using its wealth of resources to enrich your teaching. This section provides additional information to help you integrate the Internet into classroom activities.

Pages 219-222 of *IETT* describe several powerful teaching and learning strategies and give lesson plan examples for some of them. Also, the CD that comes with the text (entitled *Integrating Technology Across the Curriculum*) has example lesson plans that illustrate how to integrate the Internet into your classroom activities.

Try This! 10-1

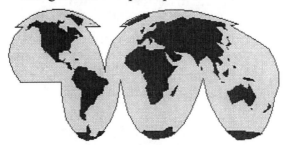

http://www.prenhall. com/roblyer

The Internet lessons on the CD are listed here by name according to the type of strategy they use. Locate each of them by clicking on the "Find Lesson Plan" option and typing in the lesson name.

Strategy #1: Electronic Penpals (p. 219)

- **A Project with Teeth.** Teachers use e-mail and the Internet to connect with "keypals" around the world in order to exchange information on how many teeth the children lose during the year.

- **Global Classroom Projects.** Encourage writing by matching students at different sites who have similar interests and having them e-mail each other about their backgrounds and perceptions.

Strategy #2: Individual and Cooperative Research Projects (p. 220)

- **Animal Logic.** Students use the Internet as one of several sources of information to research each of several animals and put together a list of traits for each animal. They use pictures from the sites to illustrate a report of their findings.

Taj, a white tiger at the National Zoo.
Photo available at the Smithsonian web site at:
http://www.si.edu/natzoo/zooview/exhibits/greatcat/ca
tatzoo.htm

- **Designing a Solar House.** Students use the Internet to gather information on the requirements of solar houses in order to design their own.

- **Online Problem-Solving Activities.** Students use online resources to practice their research and problem-solving skills in the context of curriculum objectives.

- **Thinking Critically About Information.** Describes and illustrates a model for having students do information searches and analyze and use the results.

Strategy #3: Electronic Mentoring (p. 220)

- **Gathering Information by e-mail.** Teachers and students supplement the materials and information available in the classroom by using e-mail to gather information from experts.

Strategy #4: Electronic Field Trips (p. 220)

- **A Virtual Tour of Museums.** Students look at museum tours available on Internet web sites for various museums. Then they create their own virtual tour.

"Yellow Calla" by Georgia O'Keeffe
from the Smithsonian Art Museum collection at:
http://www.nmaa.si.edu/

- **Three Days in Munich via the Internet.** Students supplement and enhance their learning of a foreign language by planning a three-day "visit" to a foreign city via Internet web sites.

- **Virtual Field Trips.** Students plan a trip to a site by visiting web sites with maps and other information about it.

Strategy #5: Group Development of Products (p. 220)

- **A Newsworthy Journey**. Use the Internet to visit the web pages of popular daily newspapers such as *USA Today, The New York Times,* and *The Washington Post* in order to decide on which sections to include when creating a class newspaper.

- **A Study of Endangered Species.** After a research project, the class creates a web site of their findings on endangered species.

- **Bridges to Learning About Each Other.** Students at different sites in the country develop descriptions of interesting sites in their locations and share the results in a jointly-created travel brochure.

- **Buy Low/Sell High: A Study of the Stock Market.** Students use Internet sites to research various companies and investment funds and create simulated investment "portfolios."

- **Celebrate the U.S.A.** Students use the Internet to research information about their home state and develop a presentation to encourage tourism there.

- **Student Weather Broadcasts.** Students download or capture National Weather Service information and satellite images from the NOAA web site and use them to create their own weather broadcasts.

OUR SEAS AND OUR SKIES

OF EXCELLENCE AT NOAA

From the National Oceanographic and Atmospheric Administration at:
http://www.noaa.gov/

- **Watching the Weather.** Students practice being "real scientists" by gathering weather data, sharing it with others, and analyzing it over time.

- **Writing Across the Country.** Participants each write a product (e.g., a poem or essay) as a "verbal postcard" to tell others about some aspect of the local community. Then students communicate these products with each other through e-mail and chatrooms set up for the project.

Strategy #6: Parallel Problem Solving

- **Global Classroom Projects.** Students challenge students in a partner class to a game competition such as the NIM game. (See the "Using Draw Software in Problem-Solving" lesson in the CD database.) Students play the games interactively so the classes at the locations can be spectators as well as participants. Another option is to arrange a "college bowl" type quiz game where each class creates questions beforehand on agreed-upon categories. Each site asks other sites their own questions. This is a good opportunity to review information from topics recently covered in class.

- **Investigating the Crime of the Century on the Internet.** Students supplement and enhance their learning of a foreign language by connecting with a cooperative group in a foreign country and work together work to solve a mystery.

- **Online Opportunities for Problem-Solving Projects.** Provides descriptions of six types of activities in which online resources can be used to support cooperative problem-solving.

Strategy #7: Social Action Projects (p. 222)

- **Acid Rain Activism.** Students use Internet web sites to explore "acid rain apathy" and develop products that can raise awareness of the problems involved and suggest possible solutions.

Welcome to the

ACID RAIN 2000

Web site maintained by: Pitsford Hall weather station, Northamptonshire Grammar School, UK http://www.brixworth.demon.co.uk/acidrain2000/

Links to Internet Lesson Plans and Teaching Resources

The following are Internet links to additional lesson plans and other materials you can use to develop your own Internet-based teaching and learning strategies.

Try This! 10-2

http://www.prenhall. com/roblyer

*Enter each of these links into your browser. Create bookmarks for each site as you connect to it. Create Bookmarks folders for each category (e. g., Internet Lesson Plans), and drag in the bookmarks related to each one. (See **Section Four** of this book for help on using bookmarks.) Look for lesson plans, strategies, and resources that will be of particular use to you.*

Internet Lesson Plans and Teaching Resources

- The AskERIC Lesson Plan Collection
  http://www.askeric.org/

- Ideas for web-based lessons from the Public Broadcasting System web site
  http://www.pbs.org/teachersource/teachtech/ideaswebbased.shtm

- Art education activities from the Kennedy Center
  http://artsedge.kennedy-center.org/cs.html

- Lesson plans available from the Apple Computer, Inc.
  Apple Learning Exchange
  http://ali.apple.com/

- A searchable database of lesson plans submitted by
  teachers to the Encarta web site
  http://encarta.msn.com/

- Astronomy lesson plans from the NASA Goddard
  Space Center
  http://education.nasa.gov/educators.html

- Lesson plans, activities, and resources from the
  National Park Service to support education in geology,
  paleontology, prairie resources, and wildlife
  http://www1.nature.nps.gov/edures/

- Free bank of lesson activities and other resources from
  the U. S. DOE
  http://www.ed.gov/free/subject.html

- Teaching modules, classroom activities, and on-going
  events from the United Nations to help teach global
  issues: Human Rights, Health, Land Mines,
  Environment, Women, Poverty
  http://www.un.org/Pubs/CyberSchoolBus/

- Lesson plans and other teaching resources on a variety
  of topics from the Smithsonian Museum
  http://educate.si.edu/resources/resourcedir.html

- Lesson ideas and opportunities available from *The
  New York Times*
  http://www.nytimes.com/learning/

- Consortium to point the way to materials from federal, state, university, and other sites
  http://www.thegateway.org/index.html

- Lesson plans and other resources for middle school
  http://www.middleschool.net/

- Examples from the University of Illinois of real Internet projects of teachers and students, and the findings of researchers who study them
  http://lrs.ed.uiuc.edu/

Online Learning Projects and Sites to Help with Collaboration Among Schools

- The ThinkQuest Internet Challenge
  http://www.thinkquest.org

- The Kidlink Network to support e-mail exchanges among students
  http://www.kidlink.org/

- Intercultural E-Mail Classroom Connections, a free service to help teachers link with partners in other countries and cultures for e-mail project exchanges
  http://www.stolaf.edu/network/iecc/

- The Global SchoolNet Foundation, a site of examples of past collaborative projects and information on how to join current ones
  http://www.gsn.org

- Live interactive expeditions that students may "join" online to real places around the world
  http://www.globalearn.org/

- Site to help K-12 educators learn how to set up their own Internet servers, link K-12 educators and students at various sites, and help them find and use K-12 web resources
  http://web66.umn.edu/